LOOKING AT
PISA

BONECHI – EDIZIONI « IL TURISMO »

50122 FIRENZE – Via dei Rustici, 5

PUBLISHER'S NOTE

It is always a source of great satisfaction and emotion when a publisher, at the moment of the parting of the ways, can write a few lines to thank his staff for their hard work, dedication, and infectious enthusiasm.

Satisfaction because after settling a host of problems and queries which arose at the beginning, our four authors managed to coordinate their individual ideas and feelings. This cooperation turned out to be a source of mutual stimulation and led to a homogeneous expressive unity despite the four authors' totally different characters.

Emotion because the time has come for that last handshake and final good-bye.

The most positive result was, I feel, the fact that the four authors, aided in their mutual respect for one another's work, managed to shed their (typically Italian!) overriding sense of individuality and work together, sometimes leading and sometimes being led. This turned out to be a highly interesting editorial experiment since every text, topic, and illustration was discussed and analyzed; many times heatedly. The result is that the the authors, all professional tourguides, have come up with a language that is more human, more familiar, more friendly than the norm — isn't this proof that art and culture are really tools for joining together and shaping the differences of opinion which are bound to crop up in any group effort?

I would like to conclude this note of mine with a brief remark. It is likely that the person who acquires this volume will, upon reading, feel as though he is being personally escorted by one of the four guides all over the wonderful town of Pisa. May he fully experience her art, history, and culture in this tour which is short in time but long in fascination.

The Publisher

Pisan possessions and searoutes sailed by the Pisan navy during the time of the glorious republic.

PISA
IN HISTORY

Only scattered and fragmentary bits of information regarding Pisa's origins have come down to us, since the " historical facts " recorded by Pliny and Strabo are largely based on legend.

Therefore, the city's origins will continue to be shrouded in the same mystery that not even the great historians of long ago were able to solve. However, the original inhabitants of Pisa might well have been seamen who settled in the area of what is now the medieval city during the pre-Roman period. It matters little whether they were Phoenicians or Greeks, since no record of their wandering has come down to us, but then neither did the Etruscans manage to leave us any trace of their civilization. Roman Pisa, on the other hand, is not at all mysterious. A colony was founded following a victory won by an allied force of Roman and Pisan troops over the Ligurians. The Emperor Augustus then increased the strength of the colony which in the meantime had become a flourishing seaport. In the year 180 A. D. the city requested and was granted the privilege of coming under Latin law. The Roman history of the city thereafter gets lost inside the mainstream of Roman history in general.

In 476 A. D. barbarian tribes swooped down into Italy and Rome, in decline, never recovered. Goths and Byzantines took over the rule of the Italian peninsula including Pisa. Later, in the 7th century, Pope Gregory the Great received aid from the Pisan navy in an expedition against the Byzantines.

The Longobards conquered all of Tuscany. Actually, no blood was spilled; it would be better to speak of a peaceful blending of the native Tuscan element with the Longobard strain. During the time of Charlemagne and his Carolingians, the city enjoyed relative independence.

But it was not until the 10th century A. D. that Pisa really began to experience her fabulous age of glory and extraordinary economic prosperity. The city looked to the sea, for her fortune lay in her navy. She fought bravely against the Saracens from Sicily, conquering Reggio Calabria in 1017 and then managed to drive her former allies out of Sardinia. This clash between Pisa and Genoa might easily have been the original cause of the rivalry which grew up between the two powerful marine republics.

Conquest after conquest followed: Carthage, Bona, and Lipari fell to Pisan land and sea troops during the years from 1030 to 1035. Jacopo Ciurini led the conquest of Corsica and the final subjection of Sardinia to Pisa, whereby the Pisan state was greatly enlarged (1051-1052).

In 1099, the Pisans flocked in large numbers to join the first crusade. In the 12th century they established trading bases along the Syrian coast. The Roman Emperor of the East, Alessio Comneno, granted the Pisan merchants special landing privileges at Constantinople as well as the right to reductions in the duties to be paid.

Piazza dei Miracoli: harmony, equilibrium, and color.

Between 1114-1116 the Balearic Islands with Ibiza, Majorca, and Minorca fell to the Pisans. Archbishop Pietro Moriconi led the Pisan navy to victory in the name of the Cross, but clearly in the name of the Pisan state's political interests as well.

As a result of this and other exploits, the free city of Italy became a respected and feared power. This is the period when Pisa became the meeting place of two civilizations, the East and the West — taking on, in fact, the leadership of the latter. During the fierce struggles between the Papacy (Guelphs) and the Emperor (Ghibellines), Pisa was quick to side with the emperors, the greatest of whom, Frederick II, was particularly fond of the city. In 1241 Pisa was excommunicated for having kidnapped the bishops and cardinals who were on their way to a council meeting with the emperor. The Ghibelline party soon succeeded in dominating the Guelphs.

In 1250 Frederick died. The other Tuscan cities, in particular Florence and Lucca, joined together in an alliance against Pisa who was compelled to pay dearly for her defeat. Then on August 6, 1284 the Pisan and Genoese armadas clashed in the vicinity of the Isle of Meloria, not far from the mouth of the Arno River, and the Pisans took a terrible beating. The main cause for the defeat was attributed to the betrayal of a Pisan nobleman, Ugolino della Gherardesca, and when the political situation worsened even more, he was seized and locked up inside the Gualandi Tower together with his children and nephews.

Towards the end of the 13th century, ominous signs of political decline cropped up in the city and serious internal disputes poisoned its political life. In 1311 the Emperor of Luxemburg, Harry VII, swept down through Italy to restore his party to its former glory. Ghibelline Italy flocked to join the cause of the young Germanic emperor, and Pisa followed suit. But then two years later, in circumstances not entirely clear, the emperor fell dead near Siena. His remains were laid to rest in Tino di Camaino's sarcophagus in the Cathedral.

A view of Piazza del Duomo (Cathedral Square) seen through a city gate.

When the Guelphs managed to seize power, the liberty which had been enjoyed by Ghibelline Pisa, as well as her independent and democratic spirit, was lost. The first despot to rule over the city, Uguccione della Faggiola, was partially successful in restoring the Pisan state back to its former glory when he taught the citizens of Lucca a cruel lesson by conquering their city in 1315. But Uguccione was too much of a tyrant and for this reason he was ousted in 1316.

Other despots then rose to power: the Gherardescas, the Gambacortis, and Giovanni dell'Agnello, whose rule left horrible memories. In 1392 Pisa was sold to the Viscontis from Milan who in turn ceded it to the Florentines for a considerable sum. At this point, the flame of liberty was violently re-ignited and a revolt against Florence spontaneously broke out. But in 1406, after being subjected to a terrible seige, Pisa was forced to surrender to avoid starvation. In 1499 the Florentine troops once more succeeded in crushing their brave yet unlucky enemies. Thus,

the ancient republic, the free city state, and all the liberties so dear to the people of Pisa fell before the reality of the new times.

Pisa under Florentine domination was ruled by the Medicis up until 1737, the year in which the last of the Medicis, Gastone, died without leaving an heir. The Granddukes of Lorraine, a minor branch of the Hapsburg line, succeeded the Medici dynasty. Even today the Lorraine rule is recognized as having been positive for the whole grandduchy of Tuscany, and Pisa was no exception. But, nevertheless, life had been drained out of the city and in 1860 after the bloodless Tuscan revolution Pisa meekly joined the new Italian state.

Today Pisa is a medium-sized provincial town with a population of 110,000, 20,000 of whom are university students. Even though the sea has receded several miles, it is still the focal point of all Pisan life. The reason lies in Pisa's history which, like the sea itself, is impermeated with the taste of saltwater.

PISA IN ART HISTORY

Although the Phoenicians, Greeks, and Etruscans left no trace in Pisa, the Romans adorned the city with splendid buildings and public baths. Numerous Roman sarcophagi preserved in the Camposanto (monumental cemetery) are proof of the city's classical heritage. In addition, huge quantities of building materials were unearthed in the Roman ruins and reutilized in the construction of the Cathedral and other monuments in the city such as the Baptistry and the Leaning Tower. These stones are still visible today — on a number of them you can read Latin inscriptions in memory of Hadrian and Trajan. As far back as the 8th century, Pisa stood out as a minor cultural center; in fact, the grammatician Pietro of Pisa was summoned to Paris by Charlemagne who, more illiterate than not, wanted to employ Pietro as his teacher. But it was not until the 11th century that the city's extraordinary artistic prospects began to open up: in 1063 Buschetto Pisano began work on the Cathedral, the first monument to be built out of the four that make up the city's architectural heart. Buschetto became the most masterful interpreter of the Pisan Romanesque style which was born from the harmonious fusion of Oriental architectural and decorative motifs with Western architectural elements. This could very well have been the first time that East and West met harmoniously in the Pisan churches. Pointed arches, polychrome decorations, dark and light alternating stripes, pilaster strips, and lozenge patterns are echoes reverberating in Pisan Romanesque of the great sea voyages eastward. In Apulia, Sardinia, Corsica, Lucca, Pistoia, and Siena, churches and bell towers were designed and put up in the style so dear to Buschetto, Diotisalvi, and Bonanno Pisano. Even the cathedral of the far away city of Spalato in Yugoslavia was built in the Pisan Romanesque style. Between 1063 and 1173 the Cathedral, the Baptistry, and the famous Leaning Tower were all begun. The Gothic monumental cemetery (in which one day the young composer Franz Liszt would be inspired to write his immortal " Totentanz ") was started in 1278 by Giovanni di Simone who also worked on the Leaning Tower after Bonanno Pisano's death.

Pisan painting comes into its own right on a national scale with the unknown " Master of San Martino ", whose work slightly antedates Cimabue and Duccio di Buoninsegna — and who, in fact, may be considered the latter's rightful master. Another 13th century artist, Giunta Pisano, was the first Western painter to break away from the severe Byzantine tradition by rendering his Christ on the Cross both human and suffering. But it is in sculpture that the Pisans capture truly universal acclaim through two great artists whose very names stand for 13th century Italian sculpture: Nicola and Giovanni Pisano. They found, as nobody before them had been able to, motifs of great expressive liberty in the city's political condition and atmosphere.

Nicola Pisano, before anyone else, focused his attention on the classical heritage of his city and country. And, before any other Italian sculptor, he succeeded in conveying the classical fascination of antique statues. Thus, his Virgins look like Greek goddesses and his saints and prophets resemble aristocratic Romans. An outstanding example is the small nude figure just beneath the Adoration of the Magi scene on the Baptistry pulpit. Whether or not Nicola's main purpose was an accurate anatomical study of the human body, we still may consider this figure very advanced for its times. Nicola's son, Giovanni, was not to be outdone by his father as can be seen in his rendering of the Hercules figure on the Cathedral pulpit. Both artists were probably cause for discussions and arguments, yet they were free to work as they pleased since they lived in a city which was basically democratic and independent. The famous sculptors joined their single talents together to produce one of Italy's loveliest fountains (in Perugia), whereby creating a great masterpiece. Giovanni Pisano was the greatest example of the drama, the torment, and the human tragedy of his century, the century whose poetic expression came from Dante Alighieri and whose pictorial genius was embodied in Giotto di Bondone. Giovanni Pisano's art forged generation upon generation of great sculptors and opened the way to the Renaissance splendors of Jacopo della Quercia, Ghiberti, Donatello, and Michelangelo.

The Leaning Tower and the Cathedral apse.

THE LEANING TOWER

Few monuments in the whole world are as famous as this one. Its amazing inclination measures approximately 15 feet. Bonanno Pisano and Guglielmo started work on the tower in 1173, even though the date given in the Latin inscription to the right of the entrance is 1174 (actually, this date refers to the Pisan calendar set one year ahead). Some months after work was begun, the tower's first level was completed. Around this lower level there are columns set into the wall with classical capitals and blind arches with lozenge designs. Work continued under the direction of Bonanno who, in addition, sculpted the four bronze doors of the Cathedral in 1180, only one of which survived the disastrous 1595 fire. In 1185, the tower, having been built up to the third floor, already began to take on the architectural appearance it has today. At this point, owing to the crumbly state of the ground upon which Pisa rises, the first subsiding of the construction took place. In fact, a goodly number of buildings, some put up before and others after the Leaning Tower, lean over just like the famous tower in Pisa. Therefore, we had better set the record straight right off: the Leaning Tower of Pisa was never vertical and its tilt was noted immediately during construction. Bonanno left Pisa that year, in 1185, to go south to Sicily where a year later he sculpted another bronze door, this time for the Cathedral of Monreale. He came back to his native city only to find death awaiting him and was given honorable burial in a sarcophagus placed at the foot of his tower (it was discovered in 1820). The fact that he never saw his famous tower completed was probably a great disappointment to Bonanno.

Later, in 1198, a number of bells were temporarily set up on the still

Above: **the Leaning Tower reflected in the play of light in the Barsanti Gallery;** *below:* **at the base of the Leaning Tower, the relief with the date the building was started.**

Unusual Romanesque capital at the base of the Leaning Tower.

unfinished building. During the first half of the 13th century, serious political disorders prevented the completion of the work, as the wars against Genoa, Florence, and Lucca absorbed the best part of the city's energies; defending their liberty and independence was uppermost in the Pisans' minds.

Work was picked up again in 1275 by Giovanni di Simone, the great architect responsible for the Church of St. Francis and the Camposanto Monumental Cemetery. It was interrupted once again in 1284, the year the Pisans suffered their great naval defeat at the hands of the Genoese. By 1319 the Leaning Tower was built up to the bell chamber stage. The bell chamber itself was added on in the years immediately following 1350 by Tommaso Pisano who with delicate skill managed to blend in the Gothic elements of the monument's upper tier with the predominantly Romanesque ones of the tower.

The exterior walls are about 14 feet across at the base and about 7 at the top. The tower is 179 feet tall and every year its inclination increases another millimeter. The problem of the Leaning Tower has now burst forth in all its seriousness and we hope that work on the bracing of the celebrated monument will soon be getting underway. The Leaning Tower is one of the numerous typically Italian bell towers although several art historians maintain that the origins of the Italian bell tower go back to the Moslem minaret. Just as the Muezin sing out their calls to prayer from the minaret, the voice of the tolling bells summons the Christian believers for the same purpose. Other experts claim it was just the opposite, and that it could have been the Arabs who were influenced by the bell towers of the Christian churches so common in pre-Islamic Syria. Leaving aside these scholarly controversies, it is safe to say that the Leaning Tower of Pisa is well known and loved throughout the entire world. Perhaps the Italians are just a bit fonder of it than anyone else, since for them the tower stands for something special; it has become a symbol of their beloved homeland.

The Leaning Tower visible in its maximum inclination.

The façade of the Cathedral is the work of Rainaldo, Buschetto's last successor, who was active during the second half of the 13th century. In the upper righthand section of the central portal, a Latin inscription reading " Rainaldus prudens operator.... " may be clearly made out. Just as in most of the Pisan churches, the façade faces westwards as if in respect for the glory that was once Western civilization. The mosaics in the lunette were designed by Alessio Baldovinetti in 1467 and later restored in 1829. The mosaic in the middle depicts the Assumption of the Virgin, the one on the left St. Reparata, and the one on the right St. John the Baptist. Two superb classical columns flank the central portal, while arches, lozenge designs, and rosettes of Oriental inspiration are used in profusion all over the lower section of the façade. The upper part of the façade makes use Lombard arcading which is repeated as the major architectural motif in the Leaning Tower and on the Cathedral's main apse. The eye sweeps up a sequence of four rows of arcading which create an impressive perspective of arches and colonnades, just as harmonious and impressive as a counterpoint in music.

In the upper righthand section of the second gallery there is a smallish Oriental red porphyry columnette which was carried off from Majorca to Pisa. According to a charming old legend whoever looks at it is safe for a day from betrayals in love.

Inside the last arch on the left side of the Cathedral façade, the Pisans of long ago decided it would be the right place to give Buschetto honorable burial. In fact, the great architect who designed the Pisa Cathedral was laid to rest in a Roman sarcophagus because it was Rome and her temples which had influenced him when he was working on the imposing church. The epitaph inscribed along the top of the sarcophagus consecrates the glory of the great architect throughout eternity. The tomb, just like the Cathedral, looks towards the west in the direction of the setting sun. And nowhere else in the square are the colors of the sunset so lovely as they are here.

The tomb of Buschetto on the Cathedral façade.

The Cathedral's central doorway.

THE CENTRAL DOORWAY OF THE CATHEDRAL

The original doors which Bonanno Pisano created in 1180 were destroyed in a terrible fire which broke out in 1595. Later the Florentine architect, Raphael Pagni, was commissioned to design three new ones by Grandduke Ferdinand I. A group of Florentine sculptors, possibly students of Giambologna, carried out Pagni's design. The panels on the central door depict the life of the Virgin, while those on the side doors portray the life of Christ. Actually, the new doors are a far cry from the stylistic perfection of Ghiberti's " Door of Paradise " on the Florentine Baptistry. And they are equally far from Bonanno Pisano's severe and extremely concise style. Each panel is noteworthy for its fine perspective and its border decoration, in truth a bit heavy-handed, which is typical of the Baroque mannerist style from then on the dominant note in Italian art. On the lefthand side of the central door corresponding to the Nativity of the Virgin panel, a number of brilliant figures may be picked out, e.g. the dog, the frog, and two tiny lizards. Legend would have in that you can make your dreams come true by touching them.

The Cathedral's central doorway: detail of the Nativity panel.

The Cathedral dome as seen from the top of the Leaning Tower.

THE CATHEDRAL DOME

The dome was added on by Lupo di Gante and Puccio di Gadduccio in the year 1380 at the height of the Gothic period. It is particularly noteworthy for its unusual elliptical shape. The dome rests upon an octagonal drum set off by a delicate yet stately encircling gallery. Nevertheless, the Romanesque complex below has in no way suffered from this slight stylistic modification. Here Italian Gothic, for the second time after the Baptistry, makes its shy appearance.

THE ST. RANIERI DOOR

When Bonanno Pisano was forced to abandon work on the Leaning Tower, he turned his attention to sculpting the set of four wonderful portals for the Cathedral. The three façade doors were completely destroyed in the 1595 fire, whereas the fourth, named for St. Ranieri since it opens into the chapel dedicated to the saint, survived and is still in excellent condition today. The work is of great artistic value and even though it lacks that "finished" slickness, it is nevertheless full of poetry and purity. Byzantine influence is strongly felt in the severe, ascetic-looking figures set into each panel. But in the Nativity, Flight into Egypt, and Crucifixion scenes, it is easy to pick out the humanity, poetic sense, and drama foreshadowing the realistic feeling which characterizes the second period of Italian medieval sculpture.

The St. Ranieri door at the point where the transept intersects the nave.

The St. Ranieri door by Bonanno Pisano.

The St. Ranieri door: Flight into Egypt panel.

The emblem of the Pisan diocese.

The emblem of the Pisan diocese.

THE CATHEDRAL

The Cathedral, the first of the four monuments in Piazza dei Miracoli to be started upon, was begun in 1063. It went up probably on the site where the Emperor Hadrian's palace and later the Church of Santa Reparata once stood. The Cathedral was consecrated by Pope Gelasius II in 1118.

Buschetto was the first of the Cathedral's architects. A Pisan, he had previously worked in Rome. During the second half of the 13th century work was picked up again and terminated by Rainaldo who was responsible for pushing out the church front and at the same time erecting the stupendous façade. The building was completed approximately two centuries after it had been started. The Cathedral of Pisa, a superb and grandiose double-aisled church, has come down to us as one of the most beautiful in all of Christendom. Its great size was most unusual for its time, and may be considered a living symbol of the Pisans' great religious fervor and the economic power of their republic.

Romanesque civilization in Italy triumphed and became identified with the Cathedral of Pisa. The full, rounded Romanesque arches and the slender, harmonious gallery of evident Lombard influence, blend in an insuperable harmony of lines, marbles, and colors, with pilaster strips and lozenge designs, and with pointed, Islamic-inspired arches and the polychrome decoration of alternating black and white bands.

The Cathedral is one of the rare Italian churches having double aisles like the basilicas of ancient Rome. However, the huge basilican shape of the church is crossed sideways by a new element, i.e., the transept, which creates the shape of a Latin cross. The imposing granite columns supporting the arcade were carried off from Palermo as spoils of war. They come from Palermo's most important mosque destroyed by the militia of the Pisan Marine Republic in 1063.

The carved wooden ceiling replaces the original one which was destroyed in the 1595 fire. It is certainly an outstanding piece of work, but it clashes too much with the simple, stately lines of the Pisan Romanesque style.

The painting inside the dome depicting the Assumption of the Virgin is by Orazio Riminaldi. The artist never had time to finish his work since he died of plague in 1631.

Cathedral: interior.

THE PULPIT IN THE CATHEDRAL

The most important work of art inside the Cathedral is the pulpit sculpted by Giovanni Pisano between 1302 and 1310. Giovanni definitely came under the influence of the Gothic style which from the north spread all over Europe; as a matter of fact, several art historians feel that he actually worked in France for some years. Nonetheless, Giovanni never forgot his origins. In this second period of Italian medieval sculpture, he knowingly managed to express to the world the ardent, passionate, and, due to historical circumstances, tragic nature of a whole city, country, and maybe even a people. With the advent of Giovanni Pisano, new horizons were opened up to Italian sculpture, i.e., all roads leading to the Renaissance were, once and for all, left free. Accentuating even more the expressive liberty his father Nicola loved so much, Giovanni Pisano created the magnificent figure of Hercules which is as completely pagan as it is nude. Perhaps no one before Giovanni was able to express himself in such terms. This is why it can be safely stated that Giovanni Pisano, the favorite son and pupil of the equally great Nicola Pisano of Baptistry Pulpit fame, set the way for the daring new naturalistic school, thus thrusting himself ahead of his time right up to the threshold of the Renaissance. And it is evident that Giovanni's realism is attained through the use of light and shadow contrasts charged with great dramatic tension and carried out with such immense skill that the artist has always been considered one of the greatest of the Italian (and European) sculptors. During the following centuries, Giovanni's intensely pursued search for content will turn up again and again as the keynote in the works of Jacopo della Quercia, Donatello, and Michelangelo.

The upper part of the pulpit consists of nine panels illustrating stories from the New Testament. The first panel depicts the Annunciation and the Visitation, and above, the Birth of St. John the Baptist. The second one shows the Nativity of Christ and the third the Adoration of the Magi, while the fourth panel illustrates the Presentation at the Temple and the Flight into Egypt. The fifth panel represents the Massacre of the Innocents. The Passion of Christ, initiated in the sixth panel, ends in the seventh with the Crucifixion. The eighth and ninth are filled with Last Judgment scenes. The lower section is largely composed of allegorical figures representing the virtues and credos of the Catholic faith. The torment, drama, and tragedy of Giovanni Pisano have been given confirmation in the world of today which is so very tormented, dramatic, and tragic.

Just a few months before starting on his magnum opus, Giovanni was commissioned by the Scrovegni family, noblemen from Padua, to sculpt the figure of a gentle Virgin Mary. There in Padua Giovanni was able to make the acquaintance of two men who would soon stand out as greats in their respective fields: Giotto di Bondone, painter, and Dante Alighieri, writer and poet.

Pulpit by Giovanni Pisano.

THE PULPIT: THE NATIVITY PANEL

In this panel Giovanni Pisano attains great expressiveness conveyed with a sensitive, highly competent hand. Pisano endows his portrayal of the Virgin with a maternal look of infinite tenderness and sweetness towards her Son, thus revealing the artist's involvement in the human drama of Christ. Giovanni did not limit his attention solely to telling the Nativity story, as can be noted in his rendering of the lowly shepherds' awestruck reactions. The goodness of this simple folk is expressed in the dialogue of the shepherds who are overcome with astonishment before the great event, the birth of the Savior. In the silence of the sculpted night, a few humble shepherds serve as examples of great purity and humility in this masterpiece by Giovanni Pisano.

THE PULPIT: THE CRUCIFIXION PANEL

In this panel all the torment and tragedy of Giovanni's own soul, as well as of his people and country, are revealed. The sense of drama is communicated in large part by the anatomical emphasis given to Christ's body and the placement of the group of women, dominated by the Virgin overcome with suffering, beneath the Cross. The influence of French Gothic sculpture is felt in the artist's highly personal treatment of this very human drama.

THE PULPIT: THE CARYATID FIGURES

This well-known marble group depicting a woman borne by four caryatid figures while breast-feeding two infants is to be interpreted as an allegorical representation of the church: the personification of the church is giving life to the Old and New Testaments represented by the two children at her breast, while the caryatid figures stand for the four cardinal virtues. The artist's treatment of the allegory reveals a realism which is strictly Tuscan — the sobriety of the composition, the rhythm of the spaces, and the the monumentality of the figures recall Giotto's wonderful frescoes. Thus, the decorative part of the group is reduced to insignificant patterns which get lost in the vigorous, self-assured treatment of the famous marble figures. The group vibrates with life and spirituality, a sign of the artist's deep understanding of both sculptural and theological matters. We can only add that here Giovanni Pisano is way ahead of his times, foreshadowing Donatello and Michelangelo.

GALILEO'S LAMP

Midway down the nave hangs a cast bronze lamp executed by Vincenzo Possenti in 1586 after a design by G. B. Lorenzi. It is commonly known as " Ga- lileo's lamp, " since it is believed that the great scientist figured out the law of pendulum movement by observing the lamp as it swang back and forth.

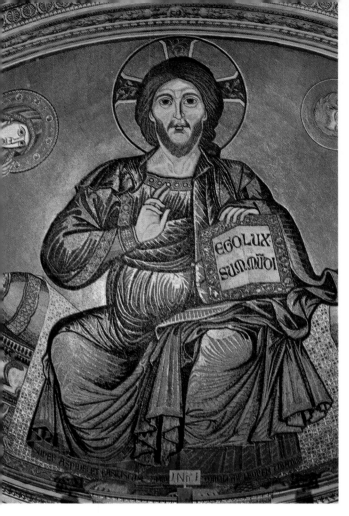

Christ Enthroned.

THE MOSAICS

The mosaic in its breathtaking gr᷍   sity is reminiscent of the Venetian and Sicilian ᷍   litions in this
artistic field. The latter in particular must have
greatly influenced the numerous artists who worked
on the mosaics in the Pisan Cathedral. The composition is rigid and contained in the best Eastern tradition and conveys that sense of mystery and spirituality which is typical of a large portion of medieval
painting. This is borne out by the figure of the Christ
Pantocrater which, set amidst elaborate decorative
motifs, is the undeniable center of attention. The
refined treatment of the mosaic is outstanding for
its rich color scheme and strong contrasts of light
and shadow. The figure of St. John the Evangelist
on the right has been attributed to Cimabue. Unfortunately, the work suffered damage in the Cathedral fire of 1595.

St. John the Evangelist attributed to Cimabue.

THE VIRGIN
AND CHILD

The Tuscan Mannerist Antonio Sogliani (1491-1544) painted this version of a typical Raphaelesque subject, treating it with typical Raphaelesque sweetness and refinement.

ST. AGNES

This is one of the most important and famous paintings inside the Cathedral. All of the elements characteristic of Renaissance painting are given emphasis here: line, color, and atmosphere. Andrea del Sarto was a careful observer of Leonardo's technique, yet he never failed to add a personal touch to great technical skill. The poet Robert Browning dedicated a famous book to St. Agnes.

THE TOMB OF HARRY VII OF LUXEMBURG

The finest example of funerary art in the Cathedral is the tomb sculpted by Tino di Camaino for Emperor Harry VII of Luxemburg. The subjects of the sarcophagus reliefs derive from classical themes previously utilized by Giovanni Pisano who in turn had followed in the footsteps of his father, Nicola. The high relief of the figures and the strong contrast of light and shadow created by the movement of the twelve Apostle figures reveal the origins of this artist who is generally classified as the most faithful follower of the Pisan school.

Harry VII was proclaimed Emperor of Luxemburg in 1308. Two years later he took a trip to Italy, at which time Pisa became his favorite city. Thus, when he died in Buonconvento near Siena in 1313, he was taken back to Pisa for burial. Dante even mentioned the melancholy young emperor in the Paradise section of the *Divine Comedy*. In the niche above, there are two refined angels by Domenico Ghirlandaio.

THE URN OF ST. RANIERI

The mortal remains of the patron saint of Pisa, St. Ranieri, have been collected in the big urn behind the altar in the chapel dedicated to him. The saint, who died in 1161, is still fervidly worshipped by the people of Pisa. Up until 1591 his remains had been preserved in a more modest sarcophagus; the one currently in use was sculpted in 1688 by G. B. Foggini. It is made of precious marbles donated by Cosimo III, the grandduke of Tuscany, and the grandduchess, Vittoria della Rovere. Every year, on June 17, the anniversary of the death of St. Ranieri, the urn is opened and the relics displayed for the veneration of the faithful.

Aerial view of Piazza del Duomo.

THE BAPTISTRY

The Baptistry is a grandiose circular building with a circumference of approximately 348 feet. If the statue of St. John the Baptist is counted, it turns out be several feet higher than tne Leaning Tower. 34,000 Pisan families taxed themselves in order that the world's biggest baptistry be built. It was a common Italian custom to erect the baptistry separate from the main church building, possibly because those who were not entitled to set foot inside the catecumenes, were not entitled to set foot inside the holy building. Our information regarding the various stages in construction is rather sketchy. On the other hand, the great differences between the Romanesque and Gothic styles on the building's exterior lead us to think that the work was carried out off and on over a long period of time. It is certain that the first architect was Diotisalvi who in 1153 drew up plans and laid the foundations of the building. The Gothic decoration on the outside has been attributed to Giovanni Pisano who is known to have worked on the building between 1277-1284. The columns on either side of the main doorway are of classical inspiration unlike the other two small columns farther in which are of Byzantine derivation. Unknown Sicilian master craftsmen carved the architrave and the small panels set on either side of the doorway. Interesting are the representations of the months of the year in a simple expressive style.

THE INTERIOR
OF THE BAPTISTRY

" 1053 Mense Augusti fundata fuit haec.... " reads the inscription on the first pilaster to the right of the Baptistry entranceway. The name " Diotisalvi magister.... " may be found instead on the first pilaster to the left. In the center stands the stupendous Baptismal Font which was sculpted and set up by Guido Bigarelli da Como in 1246. The octagonal shape of the font seems to be in contrast to the perfectly circular form of the Baptistry which, incidentally, is the sole example of a round baptistry to be found anywhere in Italy. Children used to be baptized there by immersion in accordance with an old custom whereas adults were immersed in the huge central basin. Nowadays the font is still in use, but the modern rite calls for sprinkling. Bigarelli's font is embellished with marvelous marble inlays which may be admired in perfect condition on the outside of the work. The statue of St. John the Baptist in the middle of the font is a fine contemporary work by Italo Griselli. Thus the 20th century too has left its mark in the Baptistry of Pisa. The acoustical effect produced by the dome's perfectly round shape is of great interest. A demostration may be requested of the Baptistry guard.

THE BAPTISTRY PULPIT

This pulpit was carved by Nicola Pisano. Although the great sculptor's origins are a hornet's nest of controversy, we know for sure that he was born sometime early in the 13th century and that he died after 1278. His masterpiece, the pulpit in the Pisa Baptistry, was sculpted between 1255 and 1260. And no matter where Nicola Pisano was born, Pisans are proud to call him " Sculptore de Pisis " for it was only in Pisa that he reached his extraordinary artistic maturity. " Masterpiece " does not entirely do justice to the pulpit which seems to embody the very spirit of the man who would be called " the greatest innovator of Italian sculpture. " No one before Nicola was able to give such a meaningful, and thus in effect Renaissance, sense to the art of sculpture: while at the same time other Romanesque artists were in large part closely tied and subordinate to architecture, Nicola Pisano removes his figures from the Romanesque sphere by endowing them with life and movement and thus a completely new spirit. Love for his country, the unforgettable grandeur that was Rome and thus his own city " Colonia Julia obsequens " were the factors which drove Nicola to passionately study the classical forms of Roman sculpture. For this reason the Virgins carved by Nicola's hand recall the majestic matrons and goddesses of ancient Greece and Rome, especially in the first two panels of the pulpit which depict the Nativity and the Adoration of the Magi scenes.

Just below, between the two panels, the nude male figure standing on top of the capital, is a detail of huge interest. This figure representing Hercules was not meant by

Pulpit: panel of the Presentation at the Temple.

Pulpit: Adoration of the Magi panel.

the sculptor to be an accurate anatomical study of the human body, since evidently the time was not as yet ripe. But Nicola was clearly attempting to express himself in a new way, in a way no one else before him had ever done, and even today his maturity and freedom of expression provoke reactions of wonder in the viewer. The other panels representing the "Presentation at the Temple," the "Crucifixion," and the "Last Judgment" are equally outstanding and it stands to reason that seven hundred years later Nicola Pisano's greatness still lives on. Nicola, like the man of today, was constantly caught up in attempts to say and create something new using the greatest freedom of artistic expression. Nicola makes sculpture look different because he really has something new to say, just like the great artists who will follow in his iconoclastic footsteps: Giovanni Pisano, Jacopo della Quercia, Donatello, and Michelangelo.

THE PULPIT: THE NUDE HERCULES

That classical art had an enormous influence on both the personality and art of Nicola Pisano is borne out in full by this "anatomic" Hercules. With his instinctive love of freedom as a citizen of a free republic, Nicola defies his own times by not heeding the attempts to render the world around him colorless and static. It is Nicola's limpid, serene outlook which will dominate, unopposed, the 13th century. With his Hercules, the great sculptor deliberately returns to classical forms by echoing the motifs of the archeological remains he had so lovingly studied, especially in the Phaedra Sarcophagus and the big Greek Baccanal Vase, both in the Camposanto. Thus, the reverent superstitions surrounding the pagan world fell away way forever while at the same time an enormous stimulus for advancement in the Italian, cultural and perhaps European, Middle Ages was exerted. Without heeding his critics and mindless of controversy since no great mind purposely seeks out controversy, Nicola Pisano created his Hercules to cry out to the world his free spirit i.e. the great cultural independence of a lively, restless, and modern mind.

Above: **Virgin and Child;** *below:* **St. Matthew; both works by Nicola and Giovanni Pisano.**

THE BUSTS AROUND THE BAPTISTRY

A number of years ago some of the oversized busts representing saints and prophets, originally part of the Baptistry's external decoration, were moved inside the Baptistry. They were carved by Nicola and Giovanni Pisano and others between 1250-1269 from stone quarried at San Giuliano, a town right near Pisa. It is a simple matter to pick out Nicola and Giovanni's skilled hands in the powerful expressiveness the busts display. At first glance the figures seem to be dreadfully out of proportion, but this was done on purpose since they were meant to be viewed from a minimum distance of 40-50 yards. That is why from close up the effect is a bit starteing.

THE ETRUSCAN LION

The origins of the lion set atop the Medicean walls are shrouded in mystery. Some art historians claim that the work is definitely Etruscan, while others feel that it is an Oriental-influenced Romanesque piece. What is certain is that the impressive strength of this lion figure revealed by its powerful lines and great size suggests the fabulous age when economic well-being and trade were the keynotes of the city's (and state's) political life.

THE JEWISH CEMETERY AND SYNAGOGUE

Once upon a time there was a Jewish cemetery in the Porta Nova neighborhood, but starting from the 18th century, the Jewish community took up burying their dead in this corner of peace and quiet. Pisa's name was both respected and feared in the far off Oriental lands during the Middle Ages, and naturally numerous Pisans had dealings with the Jewish communities in these countries. Documents indicate that the first Jews actually living in Pisa settled along the secluded " Chiasso dei Giudei " (" Street of the Hebrews ") starting from 1165. Then during the 14th and 15th centuries, the Pisan Jews grew very important in the city's financial world as bankers and in 1492 Jews fleeing from the Spanish Inquisition could find refuge in Pisa. The next centuries witnessed even greater advances;

Interior of the Synagogue.

in fact, by the late 19th century the Pisan Jewish community numbered approximately one thousand. Active in both the business and intellectual circles of the city, the Pisan Jews gave strong impetus to industries, especially the textiles branch. Renowned scientists belonging to the Jewish community of Pisa were acclaimed by the Italian state for their great contributions to the whole country. Only under Fascism did the racial laws lead to the break up of the community, and it was a terrible loss for the whole city. Today there is only a tiny religious community of 120 Jews who are faithful guardians of a heritage and religious tradition they are deeply proud of. Here in the synagogue Pisan Jews have been coming to meditate and pray for over two hundred years.

THE CAMPOSANTO MONUMENTAL CEMETERY

The last monument in chronological order to go up in Piazza dei Miracoli was the Monumental Cemetery, called " Camposanto " in Italian. The architect entrusted with the project, Giovanni di Simone, began work in 1278. Here, along the roofed-in passageways, the most-deserving and best-known Pisans receive burial even today. Work was broken off in 1284 because of the war against Genoa which led to the grave naval defeat of August 6 of the same year. Giovanni di Simone, like thousands of other Pisans, met his death in the tragic battle and thus found a final resting place in the Mediterranean Sea not far from his beloved city. Therefore, the Camposanto was finished much later when the Gothic style had already been deprived of its original purity. In 1464, once the ornamentation was added onto the arcading, the construction was finally completed. On July 27, 1944 two foreign armies fighting a war begun a long time before came to arms in Pisa and the ensuing battle was bitter and hard-fought. Men from countries with different cultural backgrounds coming from other civilizations did not realize the universal importance of the monuments in Piazza dei Miracoli. That day angry artillery shots were aimed at the Camposanto and the resulting damage was enormous. The roof was totally destroyed and, in the huge fire started by cannon shots which followed, the lead roofcovering melted and seeped down through the frescoes. These frescoes, which had made the Camposanto famous, were seriously damaged. It looked as though the noble Camposanto which had been a source of inspiration to Christina of Sweden, Franz Liszt, and Theophil Gauthier among other greats, would be lost forever. Italian and foreign artlovers were heartbroken at the loss of the world famous monument. And so, in 1945, a huge restoration project aimed mainly at fixing up the frescoes was set up and went on practically until today. By now it is easy to see that the Camposanto is once more as it had been before.

Although the famous frescoes were started in 1360, the cycle was completed only three centuries later. The fresco technique is the Italian invention for decorating big areas like walls. The first step in the process is to coat the wall with a layer of lime mixed with coarse-grained sand. Then another layer of lime, this time with fine-grained sand mixed in, is placed on top. On this second layer, the preliminary drawing called the " sinopia " is sketched in. The last step is the addition of color to a third layer of thick lime and fine-grained sand which gradually covers the sinopia outline. It is obvious that the latter disappears from view leaving only the fresco itself showing. After the terrible experience the frescoes went through during the war, they were detached from the walls by means of a new, avantgarde technique.

Detaching Frescoes – First of all, an extremely thin layer of canvas treated with animal glue solubile in very hot water is applied to the fresco. After a preliminary drying out period, the canvas is literally torn away, hence the name of this process which is known as the " tearing technique. " Together with the canvas, the first layer of color is also detached. Clearly in this case we cannot see the color since only the reverse side is facing out at us. Therefore, the fresco which has undergone this treatment is then placed on huge panels made of eternit braced by wooden supports and covered with extremely fine cotton gauze. This eternit is a modern prefabricated material composed of cement and abestos which does not react either chemically or mechanically. The canvas containing the fresco is first pasted on these eternit panels using cold glue and then removed with a solvent solution. Thus, the fresco is once more visible. The sinopias, or preliminary drawings, often reappear when the fresco is being torn off the wall. These sinopias are of the greatest importance since practically all of them were executed by the master himself, whereas all the frescoes barring none, are the work of pupils. It cannot be denied that the liberty of expression, the purity of line, and extraordinary dynamism which animate the preliminary sketches are tangible proof of the high level attained by the art of painting. Thus, during the final restoration, the Camposanto sinopias were detached by the same technique as the one used on the frescoes so that they could be enjoyed by sightseers and art historians alike in the halls of the monumental cemetery.

The Baptistry seen from the Camposanto.

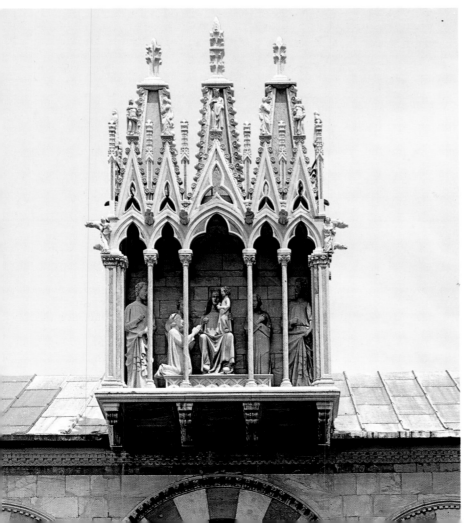

THE CAMPOSANTO TABERNACLE

A delightful Gothic decorative note in the Camposanto, the tabernacle breaks up the all too regular rhythm of the huge construction. Inside there are representations of the Virgin enthroned among four saints and a kneeling donor figure in an adoring pose. The work, which dates from the second half of the 14th century, might be from the hand of one of Giovanni's followers, as it is so reminiscent of the great master's inimitable graceful style.

On the following page: **the interior of the Camposanto.**

45

THE FRESCOES

Not all the frescoes are on display, as many of them are still inside the Pozzo Chapel here in the Camposanto waiting to be moved into the new museum now under construction which will house them. At present works by the following masters are exhibited: Taddeo Gaddi, Piero di Puccio, Spinello Aretino, and Benozzo Gozzoli, who was the greatest and most famous artist ever to have worked inside the Camposanto (the main hall off the north corridor is also dedicated to Gozzoli). Of particular interest are the Florentine master's sinopias and

studies. But we must go on to the next large hall to be able to experience that terrifing yet meaningful allegorical work by an unknown 14th century Pisan artist which illustrates the Triumph of Death, the Last Judgment, and Hell. The fresco of Anacoreti della Tebaide pales with respect to dramatic effect when compared to this work. In the group of three frescoes the medieval drama unfolds in all its tragedy. Everything is animated by religious fervor and by such a pessimistic outlook on life that it is shocking to look at them even now: first, Death not Life triumphs over the destiny of man. Then man must stand to be judged in the Last Judgment to receive his eternal reward or punishment. Lastly, punishment naturally brings on the apocalyptic vision of Hell with its endless suffering and pain.

THE SMILING VIRGIN

In this stupendous group by Giovanni Pisano, the Virgin smiles at her Son in a tender dialogue that has no equal in all of Christian iconography. Note that the Child is held in the Virgin's right arm rather than, as is more usual, in the left. The Virgin's loving glance and solemnity as she smiles and looks at her Son combined with the delicacy of the Child's glance as he smiles back at her are the elements which make this work so effective. Giovanni Pisano's deepest feelings as an artist (but also as a poet and a dreamer) are here brought into play. Only on his wanderings about Tuscany back and forth between Pisa, Pistoia, and Siena could Giovanni have found the model for his ideal mother, the Virgin Mary, her profile as finely chiseled and cleancut as the horizons in a Tuscan landscape. It is almost as if the Babe is overwhelmed by His forceful mother with the steady gaze. This work is the symbol of the artistic independence of Giovanni Pisano who so successfully managed to shake himself free from Nicola's self-control and classical dignity. The " Virgin of the Smile " signals the passing away of one kind of sculptural style; now a world of infinite tenderness is opened up, a world which is homey and familiar, yet one which never exaggerates, not even in the little joys of hearth and home. This is probably the most poetic of the great sculptor's works.

THE HIPPOGRYPH

Brought to Pisa sometime during the 13th century, we do not know whether it was a gift from an Arabian chief or else a trophy of war. In any case, this fascinating work dates from the Fatimite period.

QUESTI RESTI DELLE CATENE
ONDE L'ANTICO PORTO PISANO CHIUDEVASI
INFAUSTI MONUMENTI DI VITTORIE LUTTUOSE ALLA ITALIA
QUANDO LE FORZE DELLE DUE POTENTI REPUBBLICHE
SI CONSUMAVANO A SCAMBIEVOLE DISTRUZIONE
LA GENEROSA GENOVA
NELL'ANNO MDCCCLX · PRIMO DELLA ITALICA INDIPENDENZA
SPONTANEA A PISA RESTITUIVA
A SEGNO PERENNE DI FRATERNO AFFETTO
DI CONCORDIA E DI UNIONE ORMAI INDISSOLUBILE

THE CHAINS

This is all that is left of the chains which were once used to close off the city's harbor. Carried off as trophies of war by the Florentines and Genoese during their naval excursions against Pisa, they were spontaneously returned to the city once Italian independence was won.

Virgin and Child with Sts. John the Baptist and Evangelist, School of Nicola Pisano.

Harry VII of Luxemburg with His Entourage by Tino di Camaino.

Camposanto: the south passegeway.

Camposanto: classical sarcophagus with reliefs depicting the Phaedra story.

QVAMVIS PECCATRIX SVM DOMNA VOCATA BEATRIX

IN TVMVLO MISSA IACEO QVAE COMITISSA.

A.D.M.LXXVI.

THE SARCOPHAGI

Inside the Camposanto there are a number of Roman sarcophagi from various periods which were excavated in Pisa and placed here at the beginning of the 19th century. The most interesting sarcophagus to be found in the northern corridor was used in 1076 to receive the remains of Matilda, the Marquess of Tuscany. Decorated with Greco-Roman reliefs, the so-called Phaedra sarcophagus deserves our closest attetion. Like most other sarcophagi of the same period, i.e. the 2nd century A. D., the subject illustrated in the reliefs is of mythological origin. Briefly, the legend of Phaedra tells the story of a highly sensual woman, who perversely cast off her husband in favor of her husband's own son, Hippolytus. Nevertheless, Hippolytus never gave in to his stepmother who, furious at being rejected, then accused him of having raped her. Hippolytus was punished with death and Phaedra with such remorse that she hung herself. This typically Greek tragedy has inspired artists and writers from Euripides and Sophocles to Racine and D'Annunzio. The reliefs on the Phaedra sarcophagus give the impression of a pagan world in which Roman art is gradually drawing away from reality. In fact, by this time, we are well into the Early Christian period when the transformation of the classical world was taking place, and this disintegration meant stylized, concise treatment where sculpture was concerned. Nicola Pisano was familiar with this work and was influenced by it when he started work on his marvelous Baptistry pulpit in 1255.

Detail of the Phaedra Sarcophagus.

Camposanto. *Above:* **the Hall of the Sinopias;** *below:*
detail of the sinopia of the "Triumph of Death"
deping St. Macarius.

THE HALL OF
THE SINOPIAS

It is fundamental for the understanding of fresco painting to get
some idea of how a sinopia, or
preliminary design, was actually
made. First of all, the painter who
wanted to fresco a wall had to
prepare a small-sized sketch of what
his fresco was going to be like.
Then, he transferred the sketch in
full scale onto the lime of the wall
with a brush dipped in a red sub-
stance called " sinopia ." Bit by bit
the sinopia was covered over by the
coat of lime mixed with fine-grained
sand on which the artist or his
helpers colored in the fresco. Thus,
it is evident that the sinopia is a
highly spontaneous expression, very
free in style, and extremely alive
from a graphic point of view.

Roman inscribed slabs commemorating the death of Gaius Augustus Caesar; *right:* **Baths of Trajan, popularly called Baths of Nero.**

Portrait of Galileo Galilei by Sustermans.

GALILEO GALILEI
(1564-1642)

Galileo was born in Pisa on February 15, 1564, most likely in the working class neighborhood of Sant' Andrea fuori Porta. He completed his studies of philosophy and mathematics in the University of Pisa. It was inside the Cathedral of Pisa that Galileo, while observing the bronze lamp above the nave as it swang back and forth, figured out the law of the isochronism of the pendulum. Several years later, from the Leaning Tower, he carried out experiments on weights, proving that when two weights are dropped from the same height the speed of the fall is the same regardless of weight. Nonetheless, Galileo's experiments principally involved physics and astronomy and from 1592-1610 he taught at the University of Padua. Between 1608-1609 a device called the " eyeglass " whose purpose was to make faraway objects seem closer was in use in nearby Venice. Galileo worked on this instrument and trasformed it into what would later be called the Galilean telescope. He made a number of important discoveries studying the heavens with his telescope — he discovered the seas and mountains on the moon and four satellites of Jupiter which he dubbed " Medicean stars " after the Medicis of Florence. On March 12, 1610 in Venice he wrote and published " Sidereus Nuncius " which made public his disco-

veries and in July of the same year Cosimo II of the Medicis nominated him First Mathematician of the University of Pisa without compulsory residence and teaching duties. After eighteen happy years at Padua he moved to Arcetri just outside Florence. In 1632 he published his " Dialogue on the Major Systems " in which he expressed his agreement with and confirmation of Copernicus's theories that the earth's shape is spherical and that the earth revolves around the sun. This work is a fundamental milestone in the history of scientific thought. It was not just a simple tract on astronomy and physics but a work which served to eliminate all the prejudices and false notions held by the official science of the day and one which indicated the scientific method to be used in the study of nature and our planet as well as other heavenly bodies. The publication of this study brought on the wrath of the College of Rome which ordered Galileo to appear before the Holy Inquisition on April 12, 1633. On June 22 of that year, after having submitted to endless interrogations and threats, Galileo, at this point bitter and morally worn out, was forced to disown his work. In December he obtained permission to return to Arcetri where on, January 8, 1642, at the age of seventy-eight, he died blind and exiled.

Above: **the round weights used by Galileo to experiment on the law of gravity;** *below left:* **the great scientist's birth certificate;** *right:* **the Galilean telescope preserved in the Museum of Science in Florence.**

THE DOMUS GALILEIANA

On August 17, 1941 a law was passed in the city where Galileo was born establishing an institute called the " Domus Galileiana " in honor of the great scientist. The institute was set up to promote and coordinate study and research on Galileo's life and work, as well as to collect and preserve his manuscripts and other mementos of his life. In addition, there is a library specializing in Galileo's writings and the writings of the men who continued in the Galilean tradition. Periodically seminars and conferences for scientists and philosophers studying in the history of science are held here.

ANTONIO PACINOTTI

Antonio Pacinotti was a physicist of great renown born in Pisa in 1841. He taught in the universities of Bologna, Cagliari, and lastly in Pisa where he died in 1914. Previously, in 1906, he had been made a senator. His fame derives from his inventions of the celebrated ring device which later would be used as the prototype of the armature for the rotating direct current generator. When it was

Exterior of the Domus Galileiana.
Antonio Pacinotti's generator.

perfected it became the "little machine" experimented also as an electric generator in alternating current. Here you will find an interesting Pacinotti museum.

THE CHURCH OF SAINT CATHERINE

The Church of St. Catherine was built upon the express desire of St. Dominick around 1220 and was dedicated to St. Catherine because it was here in Pisa that she received the Stigmata. In 1311 the great Sienese artist Simone Martini painted one of his masterpieces, an altarpiece depicting the Virgin and Child with saints for this church. The famous work is now displayed in the National Museum of Pisa.

THE ABBEY OF SAN ZENO

This building, together with the adjoining Camaldolese Monastery, was already up in the 10th century. Damaged during World War II, it was recently restored. The faithful restoration brought to light its lovely, harmonious architecture dating from various periods.

Above left: **detail of the portico before the Abbey;** *right:* **detail of the façade;** *below:* **interior.**

▲ THE CHURCH OF ST. FRANCIS

The Church of St. Francis was begun during the second half of the 13th century and finished when the façade was completed at the beginning of the 14th. The building has been attributed to Nicola or Giovanni Pisano, even though there is no documentation to support the attribution.

▼ THE CHURCH OF ST. SISTO

St. Sisto is a very old, very simple Pisan Romanesque church begun on August 6, 1070, St. Sisto's day on the religious calendar, and for this reason dedicated to him. In 1786 the church was in large part restored. While the effect on its antique, simple exterior was negligible, the inside, was tastelessly modified.

PIAZZA DEI CAVALIERI

Piazza dei Cavalieri is one of the loveliest and most harmonious squares in Italy. It occupies the site of the Roman forum which during the Middle Ages became the city's political center where the Pisans used to hold democratic meetings to debate matters involving the free city state. Here in this square the Republic's triumphs and victories were celebrated, although here too in 1406 the Commissariat of the Republic announced the end of Pisan independence. Today the square retains its Renaissance appearance for which Giorgio Vasari, commissioned by the Medicis, is responsible. In 1561 Cosimo I of the Medicis, Grandduke of Tuscany, founded the religious-military order of Santo Stefano, on whose behalf the Church of the Cavalieri was erected between 1565-1569. The design is the work of Giorgio Vasari and various other Florentine architects who worked with him. It is the sole Renaissance church in a city where Romanesque is the unchallenged master. Inside are preserved several Turkish flags captured during fierce naval battles and carried back to Pisa as war trophies by the Knights of the Order of Santo Stefano. On October 7, 1571 in the Battle of Lepanto the knights fought bravely, earning glory in a battle which would prove decisive for all of Christianity. The building situated near the Church of the Cavalieri was renovated by Giorgio Vasari and the façade decorations are the work of Vasari and his pupils. The building, which was originally the knights' military training quarters, now houses the Scuola Normale Superiore, the institute of higher education founded by Napoleon in 1810. The Scuola Normale, which is totally separate from the University of Pisa, is unique in Italy in that only the best, hand-picked students are admitted to its courses. Many famous men have studied here: for instance, the first Italian to win the Nobel Prize (in 1906), the great modern poet, Giosuè Carducci, was a student. But undoubtedly the best known alumni of the Scuola Normale are the physicists Enrico Fermi and Bruno Pontecorvo who were friends as well as classmates. During the war, Pontecorvo emigrated to Russia while Fermi chose the United States. There in December 1942 Fermi successfully produced a controlled nuclear reaction for the first time in a laboratory.

Piazza dei Cavalieri. At left, the Della Gherardesca Palace with the Muda Tower. At right, the Cavalieri Palace.

The Cavalieri Palace.

The plaque commemorating Count Ugolino della Gherardesca's tragedy.

Monument to Cosimo I dei Medici by Francavilla.

THE CHURCH OF ST. STEFANO DEI CAVALIERI

Cosimo I of the Medicis, Grandduke of Tuscany, commissioned the construction of the Church of St. Stefano right over the former Church of St. Sebastian. The great Florentine architect Vasari, began work on St. Stefano's in 1565. Four years later the church was consecrated.

Inside the building there are several noteworthy works by Vasari himself (he was also a painter) and Fancelli to whom the pulpit has been attributed. In addition, there are a number of Turkish flags hung about the walls of the church brought to Pisa as trophies of war. The magnificent main altar is of great note. Commissioned by Grandduke Cosimo III, it is made of precious marbles and Oriental red porphyry. In this altar, the mortal remains of St. Stephen, donated by Pope Innocent XII to Cosimo III, are preserved and in 1427, Donatello sculpted an exceptional goldplated copper statue of St. Rossore for it. The statue is in the back part of the altar set in a niche.

The Church of San Frediano.

University of Pisa: the historic aula magna.

THE UNIVERSITY

The first Law School was already active in Pisa by the 12th century, whereas the School of Medicine was opened only in the 13th. Then the University of Pisa received the recognised of Pope Clement VI in 1343 and of Emperor Charles IV in 1350. The building at present occupied by the university was built in 1493 and later altered in 1550. Galileo studied and taught in these halls and it was here that he laid the foundations for modern experimental physics.

University of Pisa: plaque to Enrico Fermi; *below:* **the cloister.**

THE
CAMPANO TOWER

The " Campano " received this nickname from the huge bell inside the tower which rises near the food market. Since the 18th century the bell has been used to summon the students to their lessons in the nearby university.

THE ALLA GIORNATA
PALACE

This building first belonged to the Lanfreducci family. An outstanding example of civil architecture during the Renaissance period, it is now University headquarters.

THE AGOSTINI PALACE

Built during the first part of the 15th century, the Agostini Palace also known as the Hussar's Palace, is one of the oldest in the city. The building is constructed in terracotta and decorated with Gothic motifs.

The 15th century brought on greater refinement to Pisan life. Elegant palaces symbolizing the new times replaced the old fashioned tower houses which stood for strength and solidity — the Agostini Palace, as we mentioned before, was one of the first of these new style residences to go up. Recently restored, the palace still exhudes its old splendor; its serene, elegant lines give the street flanking the river a particularly distinctive look. In addition, just as a number of other buildings in the city, the palace tilts to the right due to Pisa's friable ground conditions. At present the ground floor is occupied by the Ussero Cafè, opened in 1794, which has been a meeting place for generations of students from the nearby university.

PIAZZA DELLA BERLINA

Piazza Cairoli, formerly called Piazza della Berlina, is right in the heart of medieval Pisa. The old name of the square derives from the fact that once long ago people condemned to the stocks (in Italian " berlina ") were left on public view here.

In the middle of the square atop a marble column with an Ionic capital is a charming statuette representing Abundance. It was sculpted by the nephew of Leonardo, Pierino da Vinci. All over this district, one can really sense the atmosphere of medieval Pisa.

THE TOSCANELLI PALACE

This building formerly belonged to the Lanfranchi family. In the 16th century it was restored by its new owners, the Toscanelli family and some claim that Michelangelo is responsible for the façade. From 1821 to 1822 Lord Byron took up residence in the building and it was here that he wrote a part of his poem *Don Juan*. During the same time Shelley lived in a building situated directly opposite the Toscanelli Palace on the other side of the river which unfortunately was destroyed during World War II.

THE SAN MATTEO NATIONAL MUSEUM

The Pisa National Museum is undoubtedly one of the most interesting in all of Italy and possibly in Europe. A number of the works housed in it are unique in their kind — just the museum's Giovanni Pisanos and Andrea Pisanos alone would be enough to bestow fame on any museum. Of particular note are the works classified as the Pisan primitive school: Giunta Pisano and the great unknown Master of San Martino are represented by exceptional paintings. As can be seen here, these early Pisans are undoubtedly precursors of Cimabue from Florence and Duccio di Buoninsegna from Siena.

Simone Martini painted this extraordinary altarpiece in 1313 for the Church of St. Catherine. It is definitely one of the finest works to have come out of Italian 14th century painting. Another fine piece is Nino Pisano's extremely sensitive and unusual sculpture entitled the " Madonna del Latte. " Last but certainly not least, we find Masaccio whose St. Paul is a powerful work.

Below left: **entrance to the San Matteo Museum;** *below:* **the Hall of the Dacing Sculptures by Giovanni Pisano.**

CRUCIFIX
BY GIUNTA PISANO

Giunta Pisano was born near Pisa at the beginning
of the 13th century and was active between 1229
and 1254. Only a tiny number of Giunta Pisanos
exist in all the world. This particular painting in the
Pisa National Museum (which incidentally is one
of the few signed) is a splendid expression, or inter-
pretation if you will, of profound dramatic tension.
It characterizes Pisano as one of the greatest of the
Romanesque painters, and the most masterly interpreter of Christ the Man, the man who suffers with
the greatest humility and realism (Christus Patiens).

HEADLESS DANCER

Giovanni Pisano's genius bursts forth in this monolithic marble block which portrays a young girl, headless, dancing. The artist has learned how to handle his material and it seems as though he enjoys playing with light and shadow: an expression of the typical Giovanni Pisano dynamism.

CRUCIFIX
BY BERLINGHIERI

Berlinghiero Berlinghieri, the master painter from Lucca, may be considered the ideal interpreter of the *Christus Triumphans*. A 13th century artist, he looks back to the highly spiritual tradition of Byzantine art with its mysticism and stern asceticism. In the work on display in the National Museum, a strong feeling of purification and spirituality is conveyed.

THE HALL OF THE WOOD SCULPTURES

Andrea Pisano was not related to either Nicola or Giovanni Pisano. The only link between them is an artistic affinity, even though Andrea's work bears traces of the influence of another great hub of Italian medieval sculpture, i.e. Florence, where, as a matter of fact, Andrea sculpted the south doors on the Baptistry between 1330 and 1336. But the best-known work attributed to Nicola and Giovanni's spiritual descendent is the " Virgin Annunciate." The figure's incomparable elegance, her loveliness revealed in the rhythmic lines of the plain, unadorned piece, and the treatment of the Virgin herself make the work a highly emotional and stirring experience. Other marvelous touches are the astonishment conveyed on the Virgin's face, the elegant gesture of her hands, as well as the stately, effective lines of her drapery. It just might be that Andrea Pisano came under the influence of Giotto when he worked with the great Florentine on the bell tower of the Florence Cathedral. But Andrea's origins matter little; what remains is his vibrant, lively art, filled with elegance and religious feeling, and basically free from outside influence.

Above: **the Hall of the Wood Sculptures;** *lower left:* **the Virgin Annunciate by Andrea Pisano;** *right:* **the Virgin and Child with stories from the life of Mary by the Master of San Martino.**

Madonna and Child with Saints by Simone Martini.

THE MADONNA DEL LATTE

In the " Madonna del Latte " Nino Pisano is dominated by a feeling for the delicacy of form and by
his basically Gothic nature. This means: curving
position of the Virgin, dynamism of form, and a
hint of a smile on the Virgin's face. In effect, Nino
was influenced more by Giovanni Pisano than by
his own father Andrea. The " Madonna del Latte, "
Nino's masterpiece, was executed during the first
half of the 14th century for the Church of Santa
Maria della Spina. Its refined elegance is typical of
the balanced moderation of the Tuscan, and in
particular, Pisan sculptural styles. The serene and
almost gay expression on the Virgin's face and the
highly spiritual feeling of the work are revealed
through a balance of lines repeated almost infinitely
in the extremely sensitive work of Nino Pisano,
Pisa's most delicate and human artist.

TAPESTRY AND MANUSCRIPT HALL

A whole hall of the National Museums is dedicated to tapestries and illuminated manuscripts — the room acts as pause in between the painting halls. The tapestries, woven in wool and silk with gold and silver yarn, were used to adorn the walls of sumptuous palaces. A highly sophisticated craft very common in the 16th and 17th centuries, tapestry making is a typically Baroque art form. The Baroque age marked the high point of splendor for the rulers known as " Signoria " who lived in luxurious Renaissance palaces (numerous examples may be found all over Italy).

The most noteworthy of the tapestries hung in this hall belong to the 17th century Flemish and Florentine schools.

These enormous tomes on religious subjects, e. g. New Testaments and Mass books, hand printed and illustrated by master craftsmen, are called " corali " (hymnbooks). In the display cases are several 14th century miniatures.

ST. PAUL

The real name of Masaccio, the young painter active in Pisa in 1426, was Tommaso di Messer Guidi. The altarpiece which he painted for the Church of the Carmine in Pisa was dismembered and ended up in five different museums: the National Gallery of London, the Lanckoronsky Collection in Vienna, the Friedrich Museum in Berlin, the National Museum of Naples, and the National Museum of Pisa. The St. Paul which remained in Pisa is possibly the most expressive figure in the whole work. Masaccio's fertile, tempestuous artistic talent reached its fulfilment in this balanced yet forceful figure. Unfortunately, the painter's development goes no further than 1428 when he died at the age of 27.

Masaccio boldly shook off the shackles of the decadent Gothic style, imposing his art with all the ardor of the new artistic wave of which he was the leader. In fact he is considered the greatest artist in the post-Gothic pre-Renaissance transition period. While it would be hard to pick out artists who specifically exerted influence on him, we may mention the Florentine architect Filippo Brunelleschi whose way of using perspective reappears in several painters' works. The St. Paul in the National Museum, through his powerful, monumental appearance, expresses an inner charge of deep humanity which transcends the typical symbolism and idealization of the late Gothic style. The figure of St. Paul thus becomes an early representative of the realistic approach, almost revolutionary in the way Masaccio treats his subject as a man of the people and, as such, authentic and real; St. Paul in Masaccio's eyes is in the first place a man of his times and secondly a glorious saint. It is by being faithful to his own times that man can reveal the importance of his earthly journey in the reality of a dawning new age.

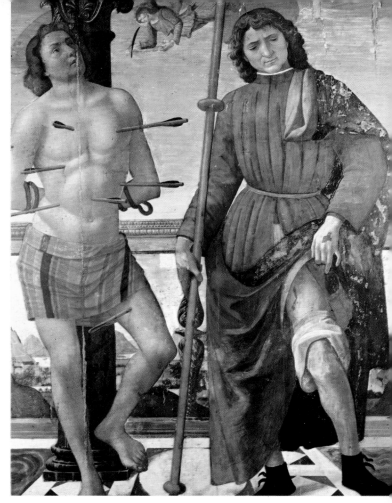

Madonna and Child by Gentile da Fabriano.   **Sts. Sebastian and Rocco by Domenico Ghirlandaio.**

Battle between Pythons and Putti by Spartaco Carlini. Probably the most talented painter to have come out of Pisa in the last hundred years, Carlini worked in his city during the early 20th century. His personality may be described as modest, simple, serene, and he was fiercely opposed to all kinds of publicity and exterior demonstrations of interest in him or his work, since he looked inward for comfort and inspiration.

The cloister of the National Museum.

THE SCOTTO GARDENS

In 1440 the Florentines, who were then the rulers of Pisa, put up their fortified citadel on the spot where today the public gardens are laid out. Then at the end of the 18th century, the land was bought by a noble family from Leghorn called Scotto. Today it has been turned into a public park.

THE CHURCH OF THE HOLY SEPULCHRE

It is believed that this church was built by Diotisalvi sometime during the second half of the 12th century for the Temple Knights. The structure recalls another building in Pisa: the Chapel of St. Agatha. As can be easily seen, its style sharply differs from the usual Pisan architectural styles.

THE GAMBACORTI PALACE

The Gambacorti Palace is undoubtedly one of the oldest buildings which adorn the Pisan lungarni, i. e. the streets on either side of the river. The building, with its attractive stately lines, is located on Lungarno Gambacorti. Its façade is extremely well-preserved considering that it was commissioned by Pietro Gambacorti, a Pisan nobleman, between 1370-1380. The building was originally topped by pointed Ghibelline crenelations which were removed during the Florentine (Guelph) domination. Above the arch of the central doorway a Latin inscription recalls the second Florentine invasion of the city.

The courtyard is of great interest. In it are preserved the remains of classical columns as well as an inscription recording the date when Cosimo I founded the Consulate of the Sea (1618).

Today the Gambacorti Palace is the seat of Pisa's city hall where the city's activities are administered. The spacious atrium of the palace is periodically turned into an art gallery where the works of contemporary artists mostly showing for the first time are displayed for the judgment of the citizenry.

THE LOGGE DEI BANCHI

Adjoning the Gambarotti Palace, (the Pisan City Hall Building) and connected to it by a passageway, are the " Logge dei Banchi " (Loggias of the Stalls) because originally the silk and wool market-place was located here. The construction was commissioned by Grandduke Ferdinand I and put up under the direction of Cosimo Pugliani after a design by the Florentine architect Buontalenti. Today the loggias are used to house a permanent art show, book stalls, and periodic band concerts.

THE CHURCH OF SANTA MARIA DELLA SPINA

Originally this tiny church was below the present level of the street, but then in 1871, owing to constant floodings, it was taken apart piece by piece and reconstructed on the new road level.

The side facing the river is the most elaborate. On the upper section are thirteen statues inside niches which depict Christ and the Twelve Apostles. They have been attributed to Giovanni Pisano. Still higher up in the niches and spires around the top numerous figures of saints and angels enrich the Gothic architecture.

The huge rose window which adorns the façade is a copy of the original now displayed in the National Museum. On the other hand, the marble group representing the Virgin with angels placed lower down in the central area is definitely an authentic piece. In fact, it has been attributed to pupils of Giovanni Pisano.

THE CHURCH OF SAN PAOLO A RIPA D'ARNO

The Church of San Paolo a Ripa d'Arno, erected around 805, is possibly the oldest church in Pisa. It is a splendid example of Pisan Romanesque, outstanding for its great architectural beauty.

Behind the Church of San Paolo stands the tiny Chapel of St. Agatha which was built after the Battle of Palermo in 1063. The delightful octagonal-shaped brick building is crowned by a huge spire.

The Chapel of St. Agatha

The Solferino Bridge before the 1966 flood.

A view of the ” lungarni ” with Medicean buildings.

The old shipyard where the Pisan galleys were repaired before setting sail for the fabulous Orient (12th century).

THE CITADEL

The Citadel or Shipyard of the Republic is now but a dim recollection of what the real Pisan shipyard was once like. Modern highways, noisy cars, and jets darting about are not enough to erase the memory of the skilful, hard-working dockworkers who, decade after decade throughout the whole Middle Ages, valiantly toiled to keep the city's fleet in good repair. It is very possible that by the beginning of the 13th century the shipyard was already in operation. Sturdy towers and walls were put up to defend this valuable place where brave sea captains had their ships repaired before setting sail eastwards along the fabulous Oriental trade routes. Then in 1406, the first time Florence conquered the city, the Florentines fortified the shipyard even better so that it would be able to withstand any attack. Finally, many hundreds of years later in 1943 the Citadel was brutally destroyed.

THE BASILICA OF SAN PIETRO A GRADO

The starkly simple church rises up majestic and solemn out of the silence of the Pisan countryside.

It is a magnificent example of a Romanesque basilica without a façade and a unique one of a church with four apses. The basilica received great veneration during the Middle Ages, since legend would have it that in the year 44 A. D. St. Peter stopped off here on his way from Antioch to Rome.

THE CHARTERHOUSE OF PISA

This Charterhouse is the second largest in Italy after Pavia's. It was founded in 1366, whereas the church on the inside was begun in 1374 and finished at the end of the century. The huge ramp of stairs on the outside was reconstructed in the 15th century and then retouched again in 1718. Set amidst centuries old trees, the Charterhouse of Pisa rises out of the quiet of the Pisan countryside, as if it alone were the solemn symbol of an epoch and a civilization.

THE ESTATE OF SAN ROSSORE

San Rossore is a huge forest filled with Mediterranean pines and other typically Mediterranean vegetation. In 1535 Alessandro dei Medici came into the property, formerly in the hands of the priests of the Pisa Cathedral. In 1789 the Lorraine Grandduke, Pietro Leopoldo, who was at the time ruler of Tuscany, permanently took possession of San Rossore. The estate in now a popular retreat for the Republic of Italy's presidents.

FOLKLORE

A city as old and as historic as Pisa could not be without its own folklore which takes us back to oldtime traditions and exciting events. Pisan folklore is particularly rich in this field, but the city's favorites are undoubtedly: the candlelight ceremony (la Luminaria), the Bridge Game (il Gioco del Ponte), the St. Ranieri Boat Race, and the Boat Race of the Four Marine Republics.

LA LUMINARIA. – Since the first half of the 14th century, it has been a Pisan custom to adorn the city's windows with lights on June 16; the evening preceding the feast-day of St. Ranieri, the Patron Saint of Pisa. Today this tradition, now a real and proper event, is undoubtedly extremely impressive. On the evening of June 16 following those typical lovely Pisan springtime days, all the buildings along the river are aglow with flickering lights reflected in the Arno. Their glitter gets mixed up with the thousands and thousands of " lampanini " which have been set on the water, giving the city a truly fairytale look.

THE GIOCO DEL PONTE. – This sham fight was originally called the Gioco del Mazzascudo and used to be held in Piazza dei Cavalieri. It mainly served to keep the Pisan youths in fine training in the arts of war. Later the game was played on the " Ponte di Mezzo, " that is, the central bridge of the city. Since the Arno divides Pisa into two parts, the southern side was baptized " Mezzogiorno, " and the northern side " Tramontana. " Knights and soldiers dressed in armor and carrying special shields called " targoni " fight to capture the bridge. Glory and honor go to the winners, austerity (" complete darkness ") awaits the losers.

THE ST. RANIERI BOAT RACE. – The race is held on June 17, the feast-day of St. Ranieri, with the various neighborhoods of the city as participants. After having sailed approximately two thousand meters (a bit more than a mile), to the finish line, a member of the crew of each boat must climb a pole and take down a flag. The winners get a cup, the losers a pair of ducks.

THE BOAT RACE OF THE FOUR MARINE RE-PUBLICS. – This historic regatta was first raced in 1956 and the idea, which originated in Pisa, has, turned out to be a big national and international success. Once every four years, Pisa, Amalfi, Genoa, and Venice play host to the boat race which is an attempt to perpetuate the memory and splendor of the old marine republics. Before the race there is a fantastic parade in historic dress to recapture the antique grandeur which, although filtered by time, is still alive and felt. On the figurehead of each boat is the symbol of its republic: for Pisa the eagle, for Amalfi the winged horse, for Genoa the winged dragon, and for Venice the lion of St. Mark.

INDEX

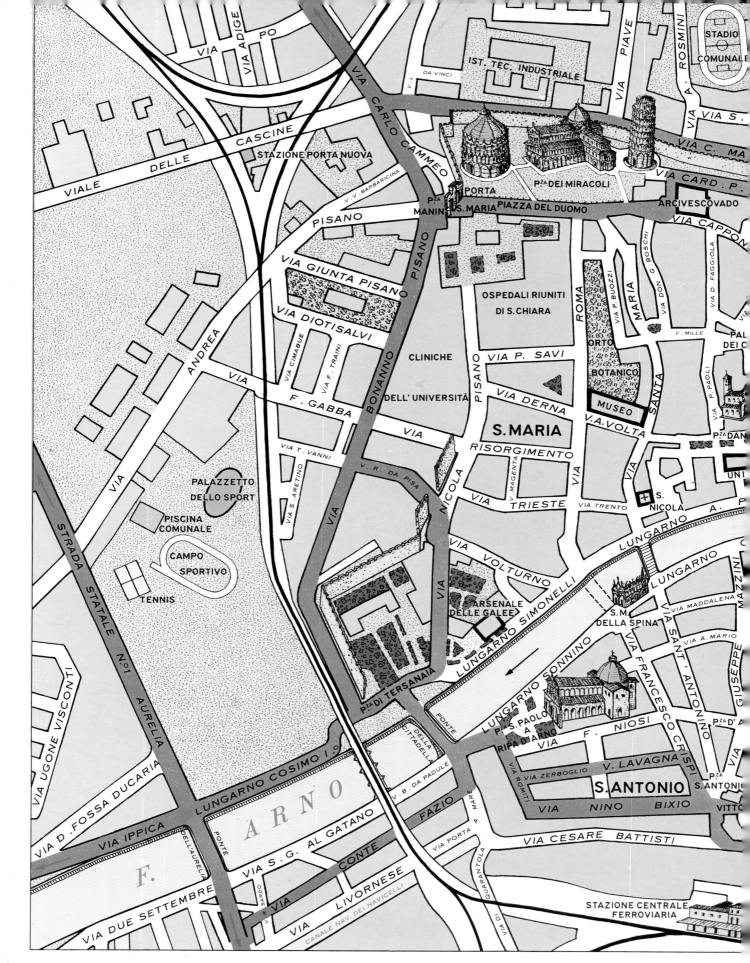

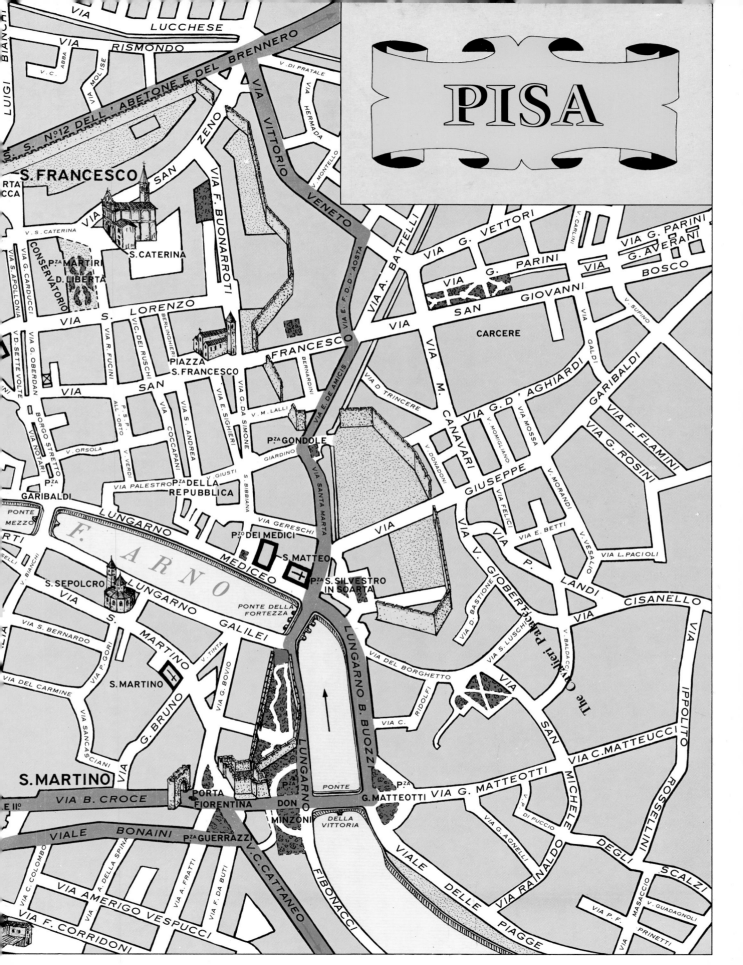

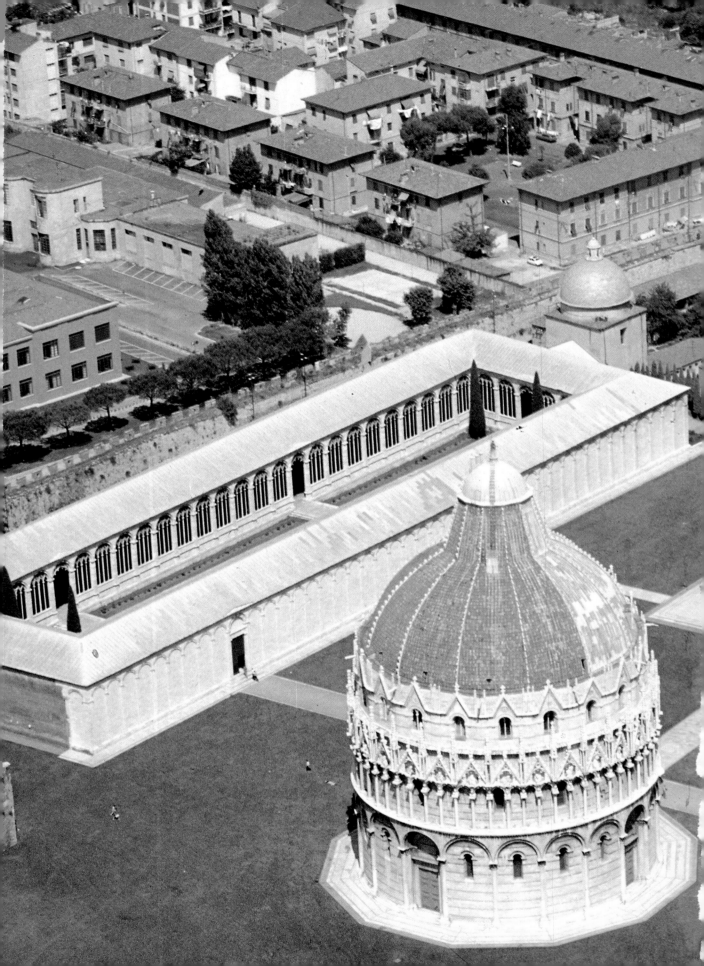

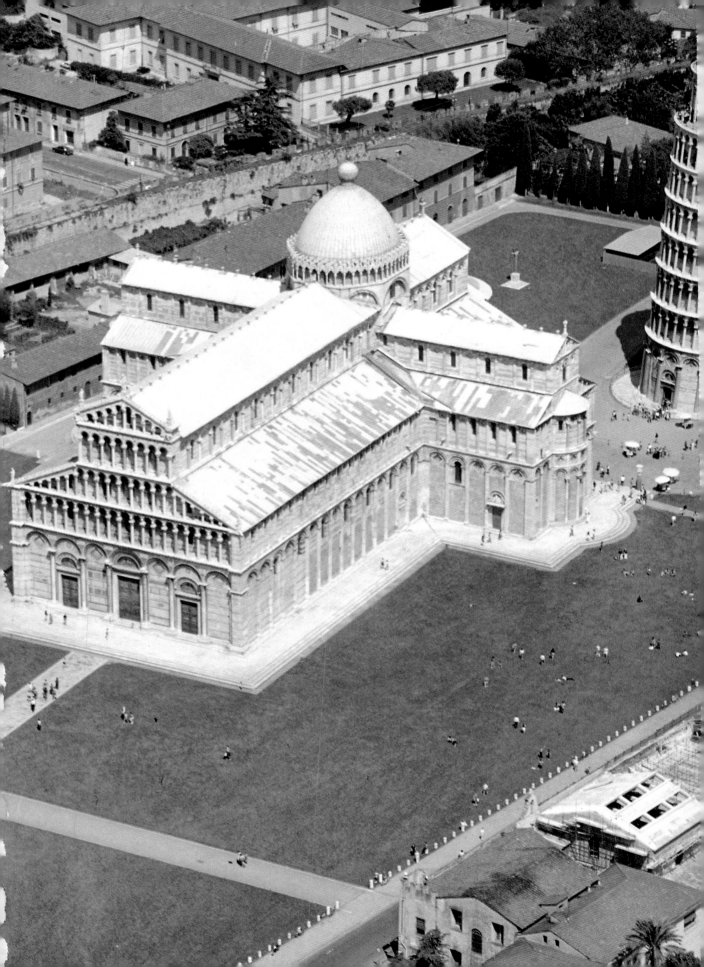